YOUR
ULTIMATE

YOUR ULTIMATE GUIDE TO STYLE

Tips, Tricks and Ideas for Getting Your Best Look Ever

People StyleWatch

CONTE

Olivia Munn

66
CHIC: CAN'T-MISS BEAUTY LOOKS

96
FEMININE: CAN'T-MISS BEAUTY LOOKS

142
COOL: THE MUST-HAVE PIECES

8 WHAT'S YOUR STYLE?

Need help identifying your signature look? Take our quiz! Answer five fun and easy questions to discover the vibe that best describes your personal style

10 CLASSIC

Effortlessly fashionable and always in style!

NTS

Rihanna

72

10 CAN'T-MISS
FEMININE
LOOKS

Jessica
Alba

CONTENTS

100 GLAM
Luxe-looking and totally standout!

130 COOL
Statement-making with an edgy flair!

160 MORE INSPIRATION
Bonus: Check out these fashion and beauty looks (and tricks!) we couldn't leave out

54
7 TRICKS TO GET A CHIC LOOK

Jennifer Aniston

52
CHIC: THE MUST-HAVE PIECES

EXTRA! YOUR STYLE RESOURCE GUIDE
A booklet with our **Ready, Set, Shop!** fashion and beauty directory; **Shop Smart: 20 Great Tips** to save time and money; and **The Best Care Tips** for your wardrobe

INTRODUCTION

FROM THE EDITORS OF *PEOPLE STYLEWATCH*

Welcome to *People StyleWatch's* first-ever style book! Our goal was to create a guide that's both fun and comprehensive, so whether you're interested in finding your signature style, reinventing your look or just wanting to try something new, you've come to the right place.

We've dedicated five chapters to the most popular style vibes: **Classic, Chic, Feminine, Glam and Cool.** (Not sure where you fall? Take our quiz on the next page to find out!) In each section you'll find fashionable celeb looks (past and present), must-have clothing and beauty items, styling tips from the pros and so much more!

But most important, we hope you'll find tons of inspiration—whatever your style—and use this book and the bonus *Your Style Resource Guide* booklet as references you can come back to time and time again.

Now turn the page and get ready to look amazing every day!

2-17-16

WHAT'S
YOUR STYLE?

Need help identifying your signature look? **Answer these
five fun and easy questions** to discover the vibe that
best describes your personal style

1. YOUR PERFECT SHADE OF NAIL POLISH IS...

a. Pale pink

b. Gray

c. Glittery

d. Gold

e. Metallic black

2. YOUR FAVE DRESS IS...

a. A printed wrap style

b. A simple sheath

c. A floral fit-and-flare

d. A sparkly tank

e. A leather mini

3. YOUR GO-TO SHOES ARE...

a. Slip-on flats

b. Pointy pumps

c. Kitten heels

d. Strappy stilettos

e. Moto boots

STYLISTS: MARK JENSEN/MARK EDWARD INC., ANITA SALERNO/RJ BENNETT REPRESENTS, SYLVIA NAGY, MARY ELLEN MEDONIS/MARK EDWARD INC., STILL LIFES, ANTHONY VERDE, ALEX CAO; ANTHONY VERDE, ALEX CAO(2); STYLISTS: KRIS JENSEN/MARK EDWARD INC., CHANEL KENNEBREW, BARBARA EISEN/RJ BENNETT REPRESENTS, CHANEL KENNEBREW(2)

4. THE BAG YOU CARRY MOST IS...

a. A top-handle style

b. A sleek black carryall

c. A pastel frame bag

d. A slouchy hobo with shiny hardware

e. A studded shoulder bag

5. THE CELEB WHOSE STYLE YOU RELATE TO IS...

a. Reese Witherspoon

b. Victoria Beckham

c. Lauren Conrad

d. Jennifer Lopez

e. Rihanna

ANSWER KEY: IF YOU CHOSE...

Mostly A's, you're **CLASSIC!**
Your style is easy, effortless and timeless. For more on classic style, turn to page 10.

Mostly B's, you're **CHIC!**
Your style is sophisticated and refined. For more on chic style, turn to page 40.

Mostly C's, you're **FEMININE!**
Your style is pretty, charming and ladylike. For more on feminine style, turn to page 70.

Mostly D's, you're **GLAM!**
Your style is bold and attention-grabbing. For more on glam style, turn to page 100.

Mostly E's, you're **COOL!**
Your style is edgy and of-the-moment. For more on cool style, turn to page 130.

CLA

SSIC

Some pieces never go out of fashion: **trench coats, pencil skirts, anything nautical.** Whether you dress them up or down, they're **forever stylish.** Sound like your kind of look? Here's everything you need to know to channel this vibe— and give it a fresh, modern feel

10 CAN'T-MISS **CLASSIC** LOOKS

Stylish celebs like Olivia Palermo, Nicole Richie and Alexa Chung show **the newest ways to wear timeless pieces.** See how they work it for day and night, and get inspired to tweak—or totally transform—your own look!

BRIGHT PEACOAT, SKINNIES & LOAFERS
Olivia Palermo's pop of color and edgier fabrics add interest to tried-and-true silhouettes.

a peacoat goes from simple to standout in eye-catching yellow

gold hardware gives a black bag a luxe feel

velvet loafers are just as comfy as ballets but up the style factor

In an Old Navy peacoat and Stubbs & Wootton loafers.

an extra
opened button
feels unfussy

**PIPED BLAZER,
BUTTON-UP
& FLARES**
Nicole Richie creates
a classic yet right-now
mix with modern
silhouettes and cat-
eye sunglasses.

a structured
jacket
dresses up
more casual
pieces

In a Saint
Laurent by Hedi
Slimane blazer,
Levi's jeans,
House of Harlow
sunglasses and
Bottega Veneta
belt with a
Balenciaga bag.

a wardrobe staple that works for the office or the weekend

a nonchalant tuck shows off a middle

WHITE BLOUSE, SKIRT & PEEP-TOES
Ivanka Trump pairs different neutral shades for a perfectly understated outfit.

a jewel tone takes a polished bag up a notch

In an Ivanka Trump top, Gabriele Strehle skirt and Ivanka Trump heels with a Giorgio Armani bag.

BLOUSE, SKIRT & PUMPS
Catherine, the Duchess of Cambridge's simple look gets a stylish twist with military-inspired details like brass buttons.

In an Alexander McQueen top and skirt.

With a Proenza Schouler bag.

SWEATER & COLORFUL SKINNIES
Karolina Kurkova pairs basics with standout coral and silver for a fun twist.

OVERALLS, TRENCH & BALLETS
Alexa Chung gives her of-the-moment denim a more traditional spin with always-stylish extras in neutral tones.

tossing it over the shoulders is a fresh way to wear any jacket

a quick cuff at the hems feels effortless

two-tone ballet flats have an Audrey Hepburn-like flair

In a Burberry coat, Topshop overalls and Chanel flats with a Louis Vuitton bag.

a frame bag lends instant elegance to any outfit

the swingy skirt can be dressed up or down

BOW BLOUSE & PLEATED SKIRT
Nicky Hilton's navy-and-white look feels sophisticated and work-ready.

In an Organic by John Patrick skirt.

white cuffs peeking out look so refined

a bright red bag is an easy way to add color

plaid is fun but not over-the-top on tailored pants

In a Smythe blazer and pants and Christian Louboutin heels with a Mulberry bag.

a peacoat in navy adds a preppy, nautical vibe

a tan cross-body offers an equestrian touch

PEACOAT, SWEATER & BOYFRIEND JEANS
Rachel Bilson keeps her laid-back ensemble pulled-together by mixing tailored and relaxed shapes.

cuffing jeans creates a fresh look

In Goldsign jeans.

In a Dolce & Gabbana top and scarf with a Dolce & Gabbana bag.

STRIPED TOP, DENIM SKIRT & WEDGES
Kylie Minogue's casual pieces get a ladylike feel in silky fabrics and feminine silhouettes.

Shop the Classic Look!

COACH *coach.com*
Find timeless leather goods, plus outerwear, watches and sunglasses that you'll wear forever.

GAP *gap.com*
Don't miss this go-to retailer for updated staples, casual weekend basics and more, all at great prices.

J.CREW *jcrew.com*
Stock up on pieces for every occasion, from easy tees to something special from the higher-end Collection line.

L.K. BENNETT
lkbennett.com
Get work-ready clothes like tailored sheaths and simple pumps—the Duchess of Cambridge is a fan!

LEVI'S *levi.com*
Check out this iconic denim brand for stylish finds like jean jackets, chambray shirts and skinnies.

RALPH LAUREN
ralphlauren.com
Shop the megadesigner's many lines—there's one for every budget!—for all-American pieces like preppy polo shirts and rugby tops.

THE MUST-HAVE PIECES

Channel a **simply stylish vibe with trenches, wrap dresses** and more—they're your new wardrobe essentials! **Streamlined shapes, neutral hues and fun pops of color** make them so versatile and right on-trend

QUILTED BAG

A black chain-strap style works for day or night

TRENCH COAT

In a wear-anywhere neutral hue, it's both functional and flattering

SLIM SKIRT

A fitted shape and knee-length hem never go out of style

STRIPED TOP

A long-sleeve tee with skinny stripes gives any look a fresh, nautical twist

LOAFERS

In brights or black, a menswear-inspired shoe is sleek enough for work and comfy enough for weekends

INITIAL NECKLACE

A monogram pendant has that special, one-of-a-kind feel—you'll wear it forever

KITTEN HEELS

They can go dressy or more casual, plus they're easy to walk in

DENIM SHIRT

In a light, medium or dark wash, it's the perfect starting point for so many classic looks

STRUCTURED BAG

A boxy shape is sophisticated and roomy enough for all your essentials

DIAMOND STUDS

They bring a gorgeous hint of sparkle to your outfit—whether they're real or faux

WRAP DRESS

A body-skimming silhouette and belted waist feel polished for almost any occasion

More Classic Must-Haves:

PEACOAT

DENIM JACKET

SHIRTDRESS

ANORAK

VARSITY SWEATER

TWO-BUTTON BLAZER

WHITE BUTTON-UP

WHITE TEE

TAILORED TROUSERS

BLACK PUMPS

BALLET FLATS

STRAIGHT LEG JEANS

Cuffed or uncuffed, with heels or flats, a slim dark pair is your go-to

MICHAEL KRAUS, STYLISTS: CHANEL KENNEBREW; URBANO DELVALLE; BARBARA EISEN/RJ BENNETT REPRESENTS; SYLVIA NAGY/RJ BENNETT REPRESENTS; KRIS JENSEN/MARK EDWARD INC.

7 TRICKS TO GET
A CLASSIC LOOK

1

Start with neutrals

"They're simple and always in style," says celeb stylist Nicole Chavez. "Plus, they work year-round." Think beige, brown, navy—the kind of colors that can be mixed and matched and seamlessly paired with more standout hues.

2

Wear at least one menswear-inspired piece

"It adds a bit of swagger," says celeb stylist Kate Young. Invest in a borrowed-from-the-boys watch in silver or gold, a tux blazer or a pair of aviator sunglasses. "Aviators are a quintessential classic," says Chavez.

3

Play with proportion and volume

"It keeps your look fresh and evolving without losing the timeless feel," say celeb stylists Emily Current and Meritt Elliott. "A white button-up is just as classic in an oversize style." Pair it with skinnies for balance.

4

Highlight your lips

"A punchy lip—whether it's poppy orange or classic red or a dark burgundy—can make quite a statement," say Current and Elliott. "Especially when paired with traditional pieces, like a pencil skirt and a button-up." Keep the rest of your face clean and fresh.

Blake Lively's furry collar and equestrian boots make the easy palette look luxe.

In a Brunello Cucinelli coat, Lorraine Schwartz earrings and Brunello Cucinelli boots with a Givenchy bag.

It's easier than you think **to master a style that's effortless yet of-the-moment.** Here we share the latest **tips and outfit ideas** from celeb stylists and more

5

Carry a timeless bag

"The right one can even make jeans and a tee more polished," say Current and Elliott. Go for more structured shapes, as well as details like top handles, in versatile hues.

6

Have fun with jewelry

"Add costume pieces," says Young. "A string of pearls or a chunky gold bracelet adds a little something extra to an otherwise simple outfit." It's such an affordable and easy way to lend interest.

7

Incorporate prints and bold hues

"Fun patterns or colors are a great way to amp up a classic look," says Chavez. Try playing with leopard print (it's practically a neutral!), polka dots, stripes and shots of red.

GET THE LOOK
An oversize watch with a leather band is a modern way to do menswear, and a pearl choker can be worn with anything.

Diane Kruger adds interest to traditional separates by mixing cute polka-dot and striped prints.

In a Diane von Furstenberg blazer, Ray-Ban sunglasses and Christian Louboutin flats with a Rochas bag.

STYLE SETTER
REESE WITHERSPO

The award-winning actress works a **timeless look** that's always on point. Sticking to a mostly neutral palette, she goes for pieces that feel **tailored yet easy,** like A-line minis, button-ups and everyday skinny jeans. **Pops of color and prints** on tops, shoes, shorts and more keep her look from feeling simple, while **sophisticated extras** like structured satchels and minimal jewelry add instant polish

TWEED JACKET
& FLIPPY MINI

ON

In a Maison Scotch jacket and
Ray-Ban sunglasses
with a Saint Laurent by Hedi
Slimane bag.

CHAMBRAY
SHIRT &
BRIGHT MINI

In Pierre Hardy heels with
a Saint Laurent
by Hedi Slimane bag.

STRIPED
TOP &
VIBRANT
HEELS

In a Club Monaco jacket
and Ray-Ban sunglasses
with a The Row bag.

"
Reese's style
is fresh
and modern
yet super
approachable.
She's the
quintessential
classic girl."
—Kate Dimmock,
fashion director,
People StyleWatch

CAMEL COAT &
BOOTIES

BUTTON-UP &
ANCHOR-
PRINT
SHORTS

**In a Maje coat and Guess booties
with a Louis Vuitton bag.**

**In J.Crew shorts, Oliver Peoples
sunglasses, a Malyet necklace and
K. Jacques sandals with a Céline bag.**

COLORFUL TEE & WHITE JEANS

In Tom Ford sunglasses and Pedro Garcia heels with a Givenchy bag.

TOGGLE COAT & RAIN BOOTS

In a Michael Kors jacket, Ray-Ban sunglasses and Hunter boots with a Saint Laurent by Hedi Slimane bag.

PLAID SHIRT & SKINNY JEANS

In a Rails shirt, Westward Leaning sunglasses and Golden Goose boots.

365 DAYS OF

Pieces that **stand the test of time** will keep you looking good

Traditional pieces like bold coats and Fair Isle knits, plus furry touches and pops of plaid have a cozy, rustic feel

Kirsten
Dunst

Michelle
Williams

Jamie
Chung

Pippa
Middleton

Elle
Macpherson

Jordin
Sparks

GREAT STYLE

ear-round! Check out these celebs' seasonal outfits

**Easy solids and stripes on everything from casual tees
to little jackets look fresh and so stylish**

Kate
Moss

Maria
Menounos

Catherine, Duchess
of Cambridge

Jamie
Chung

Ali
Larter

Freida
Pinto

SUMMER

Red, white and blue hues lend a breezy, all-American vibe
to cinched-waist dresses, lightweight tops and more

Nicole
Richie

Michelle
Williams

Ashley
Madekwe

Alessandra
Ambrosio

Julianne
Hough

Allison
Williams

FALL

Well-cut jackets, simple denim and refined layers are effortlessly sophisticated and spot-on for the season

Olivia
Palermo

Kate
Mara

Lupita
Nyong'o

Rose
Byrne

Jessica
Alba

Garcelle
Beauvais

CLASSIC LOOKS
THROUGH THE AGES

Style icons including Katharine Hepburn and Lauren Hutton **embody this truly timeless mood.** See why they're proof you can never go wrong with **a belted trench, great jeans and a pearl choker**

Farrah Fawcett
1976
In a *Charlie's Angels* episode, the star takes a spin in a track jacket, flared jeans and trainers.

Lauren Hutton
1970s
The model and actress is picture-perfect in a fitted tee and denim skirt.

Grace Kelly
1954
The actress's polished waves and single strand of pearls are so elegant.

Jacqueline Kennedy Onassis
1974

The former First Lady knows the power of an always-appropriate trench.

Lauren Bacall
1950s

The big-screen beauty's layered top and tailored shorts are polished and casual.

Katharine Hepburn
1939

The film legend is pulled together yet effortless in a simple blouse and wide-leg pants.

Diana, Princess of Wales
1994

The princess's choice of a navy coatdress trimmed in white and accessorized with pearls is so regal.

Diane Keaton
1977

In *Annie Hall*, the star does preppy with a twist in a boyish vest and baggy khakis.

a hint of blush on the apples of the cheeks wakes up skin

ALLOVER GLOW
AnnaSophia Robb highlights her features naturally by keeping her complexion radiant and adding just a touch of color to lips and cheeks.

CAN'T-MISS
BEAUTY LOOKS

Classic hair and makeup are all about keeping it fresh—
a red pout, neutral eyes, healthy strands and more.
Get inspired by these standout celeb ideas

EASY WAVES
Olivia Munn goes for a
wholesome, carefree look by
pinning her hair off her
face with a simple bobby.

POLISHED WAVES
Ali Larter's do—lustrous
texture with bouncy
movement—is always in.

SUPERGLOSSY STRANDS
Kate Mara makes her cut feel effortless
by tucking one side behind her ear.

a bright hue is a great way to take your look from day to night

RED LIPSTICK & PULLED-BACK HAIR
Allison Williams does red lips the classic way by toning down the rest of her makeup—and even her hairstyle.

SOFT HAIR & MAKEUP
Olivia Palermo nails weekend casual with a ponytail and barely-there shades for eyes and lips.

BOB WITH BANGS
Karlie Kloss's timeless style has pretty details—sideswept bangs and a slight bend at the ends.

NATURAL MAKEUP & BROWS
Lupita Nyong'o gives off a youthful vibe with full arches, plus minimal makeup like neutral eye shadow and lip gloss.

The Tool Kit
Your must-haves to get classic right—lipstick, blush, nail polish and more

CREAM BLUSH
The smooth texture looks natural and gives cheeks a flirty glow.

NEUTRAL EYE SHADOWS
Earthy tones add definition to eyes for both day and night looks.

RED LIPSTICK
The universally flattering lip color dresses up any outfit.

PINK GLOSS
An understated hue with a touch of sheen enhances lips.

PALE PINK NAIL POLISH
This pretty and quiet shade makes nails look simply well-groomed.

39

CHIC

Some pieces always look polished: **well-cut jackets, sheath dresses, heels.** Whether you dress them up or down, they're **simply sophisticated.** Sound like your kind of look? Here's everything you need to know to channel this vibe—and give it a fresh, modern feel

10 CAN'T-MISS **CHIC** LOOKS

Stylish celebs like Anne Hathaway, Diane Kruger and Gwyneth Paltrow show **the newest ways to wear sleek, elegant pieces.** See how they work it for day and night, and get inspired to tweak—or totally transform—your own look!

these 3/4 sleeves show off long leather gloves

GRAY COAT, SKIRT & PUMPS
Anne Hathaway creates a perfectly tailored mix with a cropped-sleeve coat and refined extras.

a structured shape keeps an oversize style polished

In a Marni coat, Carven top and skirt, Stella McCartney sunglasses and Aldo pumps with a Givenchy by Riccardo Tisci bag.

black tights and shoes elongate legs

a cap adds an unexpected yet personal touch

FIT-AND-FLARE DRESS & FLATS
Diane Kruger keeps the exaggerated shape sleek and not over-the-top with a simple color palette.

a knee-length hem balances the bold cut

studs offer a modern twist to ballet flats

In a Chanel dress, hat and earring and Christian Louboutin flats with a Chanel clutch.

cat-eye shades up the glam factor

a black coat in a classic shape works with everything

leather skinnies are just as versatile as jeans

TAILORED COAT & LEATHER SKINNIES

Miranda Kerr makes a monochromatic look even more sophisticated with perfectly cut separates in a mix of materials and proportions.

In a Givenchy coat, The Row sweater, Helmut Lang pants and Manolo Blahnik pumps with a Givenchy bag.

TEXTURED SWEATER & SKINNIES
Olivia Palermo livens up a casual knit staple with leather and embroidered heels.

In L.K. Bennett heels with a Givenchy bag.

In a Nina Ricci top and skirt and Kurt Geiger pumps.

PRINTED TURTLENECK & PENCIL SKIRT
Kate Bosworth goes for classic silhouettes in a graphic pattern with sleek pumps.

DRAPED DRESS & COLORFUL STILETTOS
Lupita Nyong'o gives a body-skimming dress a playful spin with bright pointy pumps.

ruching at the middle highlights the waist

a metallic clutch goes with so many looks

the pointy toes keep a fun hue sophisticated

In an Altuzarra dress, Dior Fine Jewelry earrings and ring and Bruno Magli pumps.

a popped collar offers a preppy twist

a tucked-in blouse creates a streamlined silhouette

CAMEL COAT, LEATHER PANTS & HEELS
Zoë Saldana creates a sleek look with simple cuts in luxurious fabrics.

textured leather adds interest to timeless pumps

In a Miu Miu top, pants and pumps.

LWD & COAT
Cameron Diaz's black-and-white palette lends instant polish to a peplum dress and coat.

a peplum is refined and universally flattering

patent leather gives a hint of shine

In a Chanel coat and dress.

TUXEDO & HEELS
Gwyneth Paltrow makes dressy unexpected in a menswear-inspired suit, plus subtle sparkle.

rolled sleeves feel unfussy

statement jewelry luxes up the outfit

the cropped length shows off stilettos

In a Louis Vuitton jacket, pants, bracelet and heels.

In a Bec & Bridge dress.

BELTED SHEATH & PEEP-TOE BOOTIES
Elle Macpherson goes for a fresh, modern vibe in head-to-toe white.

Shop the Chic Look!

CALVIN KLEIN
calvinklein.com
Get in on the minimalist vibe that's made this line a go-to for polished finds like sheaths and pointy pumps.

CLUB MONACO
clubmonaco.com
Turn to this brand for effortless wardrobe staples that have an of-the-moment twist.

DIANE VON FURSTENBERG
dvf.com
Don't miss these sexy, understated wardrobe must-haves, including the iconic wrap dress.

J BRAND
jbrandjeans.com
Check out its polished denim pieces, as well as the simply stylish ready-to-wear collection.

THEORY
theory.com
Find everything you need to create pulled-together outfits, from perfectly tailored blazers to dress pants and more.

ZARA
zara.com
Shop its clothing and accessories to stay up-to-the-second with the latest trends—without breaking the bank.

THE MUST-HAVE PIECES

Work a **sophisticated look with pumps, tailored trousers** and more—they're your new wardrobe essentials! **Sleek shapes and subdued hues** make them so polished and right on-trend

MINIMALIST COAT

Whether it's boxy or fitted, a simple design in subtle neutrals looks perfectly polished

MODERN CUFF

An architectural bracelet in gold or silver offers the right amount of interest and shine

PENCIL SKIRT

In a body-skimming fit, the straight silhouette looks streamlined with pumps or booties

POINTY PUMPS

Sky-high pointy stilettos in luxe textures like leather work with any look

OVERSIZE HANDBAG

A roomy, unadorned style makes for a go-anywhere carryall—a total investment piece

CAT-EYE SUNGLASSES

Retro-inspired frames are iconic—they instantly amp up an outfit

ANKLE BOOTIES

A sleek pair with little detail goes with everything from jeans to a dress

LINK NECKLACE

It's such a bold-yet-elegant extra—and it's great with tons of necklines

SHEATH

The fitted style and knee-length hem are universally appropriate—and stylish

SKINNY TROUSERS

In a just-right fit, a slim tailored style is so flattering

More Chic Must-Haves:

ANIMAL-PRINT FLATS

CASHMERE SWEATER

ROBE COAT

TO-THE-KNEE BOOTS

CHUNKY RING

WHITE JEANS

PYRAMID STUDS

SLEEVELESS SHELL

EMBOSSED SKINNY BELT

DAY CLUTCH

SILKY BLOUSE

Paired with skinnies or a pencil skirt, an easy shirt always looks refined

7 TRICKS TO GET
A CHIC LOOK

1

Go mono-chromatic

"Wearing all one color but in different tones looks sexy and sleek," says celeb stylist Micaela Erlanger. While grays, blacks and tans are easiest, brights, pastels and jewel tones can look just as pulled-together. To keep it interesting, go for pieces with a mix of textures.

2

Add a bold lip

"A strong lip color, like red, can be very chic," says celeb stylist Jen Rade. For eyes, go for a thin line of black liquid eyeliner on both top and bottom and dark mascara. Avoid dark eye shadows—they can make you look too done up and like you're trying too hard.

3

Wear statement jewelry

"Choose one bold accessory," says Erlanger. "It looks confident." Pick a piece that can stand on its own, like a triple-strand necklace, a chunky cuff or a cocktail ring. Costume extras work just as well as the real thing!

4

Pay attention to proportions

"Dressing is about balance," says Erlanger. "If you do it right, you'll always look long and lean." Think opposites: Offset a high-waisted bottom with a cropped jacket or a bulky sweater with sleek pants.

Ashley Madekwe pulls off head-to-toe color by wearing similar shades.

In a Mural jacket, Leith dress and Manolo Blahnik pumps.

It's easier than you think **to master a style that's polished yet right now.** Here we share the latest **tips and outfit ideas** from celeb stylists and more

Jennifer Aniston's perfectly tailored peplum dress is sophisticated and flattering.

In a Tom Ford dress, bracelets and heels with a Tom Ford clutch.

5

Don't forget gray

"People think of nude or black for neutrals," says Rade. "But gray is just as chic and more modern." Look for slate, charcoal, gunmetal and more on accessories or basics.

6

Pick yellow and rose gold

"There's something delicate about gold," says Erlanger. "Silver has a tougher feel." Try a bracelet, earrings or a necklace in the warmer metals—even hardware on a bag—for added shine.

GET THE LOOK
A sleek gold choker feels supermodern, and in gray, stilettos are sexy but still polished.

7

Find the right fit

"Tailoring is so important," says Erlanger. Go for slim silhouettes, like skinnies or a pencil skirt, and ones that show off the waist. Thinner fabrics, like merino wool or cotton, give you a streamlined look. Or, when in doubt, have it altered by a pro.

STYLE SETTER
VICTORIA BECKHAM

The designer and style icon has an **impeccable fashion sense** that always wows. Working mostly neutral hues and **streamlined pieces—**tailored trousers, midi skirts, fitted dresses and more—she steps out looking completely polished. The occasional **shot of rich color** adds a luxe contrast, while **sleek, minimal accessories,** like boxy clutches, barely-there jewelry, pointy pumps and slim boots, finish her perfectly refined look

PANTSUIT & HEELS

In Victoria Beckham sunglasses and Manolo Blahnik pumps with a Victoria Beckham clutch.

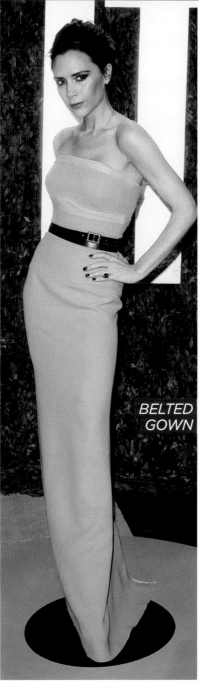

BELTED GOWN

In a Victoria Beckham gown.

STRIPED DRESS & PEEP-TOE BOOTS

In a Victoria Beckham dress and Tom Ford boots with a Victoria Beckham bag.

> "There's such an elegance about her. It's the way she throws a coat over her shoulders or pairs stilettos with a menswear pant; she radiates confidence and style."
> —Kate Dimmock, fashion director, *People StyleWatch*

COAT & ANKLE-LENGTH PANTS

MILITARY-INSPIRED DRESS

In a Victoria Beckham coat and Manolo Blahnik pumps with a Victoria Beckham clutch.

In a Victoria Beckham dress, belt and sunglasses and Tom Ford boots.

BUTTON-UP & A-LINE MINI

SWEATER & FLARED JEANS

BLOUSE & MIDI SKIRT

In a Victoria Beckham shirt and skirt and Manolo Blahnik heels with a Victoria Beckham clutch.

In a Carven sweater and J Brand jeans with a Victoria Beckham clutch.

In a Victoria Beckham top and skirt and Casadei pumps.

365 DAYS OF

Pieces that **create pure polish** will keep you looking goo

Structured coats and sleek dresses mixed with leather pants,
turtlenecks and more ward off the cold in style

| Karolina Kurkova | Queen Latifah | Gwyneth Paltrow | Kendall Jenner | Charlize Theron | Emma Watson |

GREAT STYLE

year-round! Check out these celebs' seasonal outfits

SPRING

Short suits, body-skimming dresses and tailored jackets—in black, white or pastel—make for a fresh, pulled-together look

Cate
Blanchett

Ashley
Madekwe

Angelina
Jolie

Kourtney
Kardashian

Jessica
Alba

Rosie
Huntington-
Whiteley

SUMMER

Simple warm-weather pieces—from jumpsuits to dresses—are special with ruching details, silky fabrics and streamlined extras

Eva
Longoria

Rosie
Huntington-
Whiteley

Kelly
Rowland

Gwyneth
Paltrow

Lupita
Nyong'o

Kate
Bosworth

FALL

Chunky knits and boxy coats paired with sleeker items create effortlessly sophisticated layers

Zoë
Saldana

Jessica
Alba

Kate
Moss

Olivia
Palermo

Shay
Mitchell

Miranda
Kerr

CHIC LOOKS
THROUGH THE AGES

Style icons including Audrey Hepburn and Faye Dunaway **embody this utterly sophisticated mood.** See why they're proof you can never go wrong with **a simple sheath and crisp white shirt**

Audrey Hepburn
1961

The star, in *Breakfast at Tiffany's*, is captivating in a sleek black dress and strands of pearls.

Diahann Carroll
1954

The star nails the boxy jacket, slim pant, pointy shoe equation.

Sharon Stone
1998

The actress balances a standout satin skirt with a classic button-up.

Bianca Jagger
1972
....
The jet-setter steps out in a tailored men's-style suit.

Lauren Bacall
1945
....
The film star mixes a white dress and red lip to stunning effect.

Carolyn Bessette Kennedy
1998
....
The former fashion publicist works a streamlined navy look.

Jacqueline Kennedy
1963
....
The First Lady is striking in a matching skirt set with polished extras.

Faye Dunaway
1967
....
The *Bonnie and Clyde* star on the set in a simple satin blouse detailed with open stitch work and a stylish beret.

Marlene Dietrich
1930s
....
The femme fatale actress poses in a double-breasted suit and contrasting pumps.

peachy blush
adds soft
contrast to a
deep lip color

**DARK LIP &
SLEEK HAIR**
Olivia Munn wears
a sexy eye-catching
red color on her lips
and shows it off
with slicked-back
strands.

CAN'T-MISS
BEAUTY LOOKS

Chic hair and makeup are all about polish—**a sleek updo, bold lip, stylish cut** and more. Get inspired by these standout celeb ideas

DEEP SIDE PART & LINED EYES
Emma Roberts's angular lob is so smart-looking, and black liner makes her eyes really stand out.

UPDO & RED LIPS
Emma Watson's side-parted style plus a notice-me lip color says modern elegance.

SMOOTH CHIGNON
Rosie Huntington-Whiteley amps up her refined low bun with woven detailing.

barely-there shadow plus mascara subtly defines eyes

a bold orange shade has a trendy feel

STATEMENT LIPS & PONYTAIL
Kate Bosworth's bright lip and slick low pony create a look that's fresh.

SMOOTHED-BACK STYLE
Kate Upton gives her hair an on-trend twist by brushing it away from her face.

NATURAL MAKEUP & PIXIE CUT
Charlize Theron balances pretty and polished makeup with an of-the-moment cropped style.

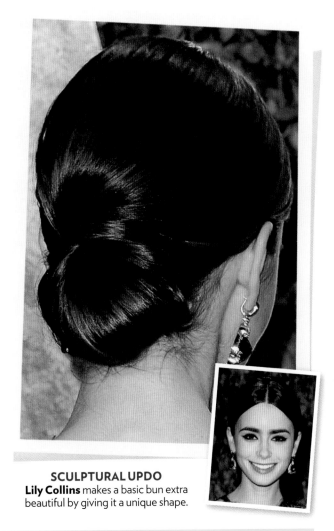

SCULPTURAL UPDO
Lily Collins makes a basic bun extra beautiful by giving it a unique shape.

The Tool Kit
Your must-haves to get chic right—
lipstick, liner, nail polish and more

NUDE LIPSTICK
Just a touch of color makes lips look finished in a natural way.

BLACK LIQUID LINER
It's the go-to for creating the perfect cat eye.

VOLUMIZING MASCARA
Perfect for day or night, it gives lashes flirty definition.

GRAY NAIL POLISH
It's an unexpected way to rock a neutral mani.

DARK RED LIPSTICK
A deep burgundy is a chic alternative to classic red.

69

FEMI

NINE

Some pieces just say girlie girl: **romantic dresses, delicate jewelry, anything pink.** Whether you dress them up or down, they're **perfectly pretty.** Sound like your kind of look? Here's everything you need to know to channel this vibe—and give it a fresh, modern feel

10 CAN'T-MISS FEMININE LOOKS

Stylish celebs like Jessica Alba, Taylor Swift and Sarah Jessica Parker show **the newest ways to wear flirty, ladylike pieces.** See how they work it for day and night, and get inspired to tweak—or totally transform—your own look!

CROPPED KNIT & FLOATY SKIRT Jessica Alba's chunky sweater and black extras offset the skirt's romantic vibe.

patent leather is unexpected yet chic on a frame bag

a cropped silhouette highlights the waist

a just-above-the-ankle hem shows off delicate heels

In a Ralph Lauren sweater, skirt and heels with a Ralph Lauren bag.

a khaki trench offers a sleek touch

a bag and shoes in the same shade are a classic pairing

In an Armani Exchange trench, Elizabeth and James top, ASOS pants and Schutz heels with a Henri Bendel bag.

the slim style keeps pink looking polished

TRENCH, TEXTURED TOP & PINK PANTS
Jamie Chung looks sleek and charming with perfectly tailored pieces in pastels and neutrals.

LACE DRESS, CROSS-BODY & POINTY HEELS
Sarah Jessica Parker keeps lace from feeling precious with contrasting extras.

pearls have a vintagey, ladylike vibe

peekaboo sleeves show a hint of skin

the color and chic shape are unexpected

In a Dolce & Gabbana dress, Mikimoto necklace and René Caovilla pumps.

a textured pattern adds a pretty contrast

PINK SWEATER, LACE SKIRT & FLATS
Emmy Rossum goes totally girlie with soft colors, delicate details and ballets.

In a Tanya Taylor top and Rebecca Taylor skirt with a Ralph Lauren bag.

the mix of colors ties the entire look together

In a Modcloth dress with an Elie Saab bag.

FLORAL-PRINT DRESS, CHAIN-STRAP BAG & HEELS
Taylor Swift gives her pretty dress a sophisticated spin with a structured bag and heeled loafers.

a knotted belt creates an instant hourglass

studded heels are dressy and offer just a little edge

In a Jason Wu dress and Valentino heels.

FLORAL DRESS, BELT & PEEP-TOES
Gabrielle Union's black-and-white palette feels elegant yet sweet on ladylike shapes.

tailored pleats and an oxford collar add interest to a white top

PRETTY BLOUSE, BOYFRIEND JEANS & ANKLE STRAPS
Kylie Minogue dresses up her denim with silky fabrics and shots of metallics.

thin ankle straps + shiny gold heels = so delicate

In Ray-Ban sunglasses.

a cropped moto lends a surprising hint of edge

MOTO JACKET, TURTLENECK & FULL SKIRT
Alexa Chung pairs an oversize floral print with tougher extras for a modern twist.

the black and white hues create cool contrast with the full shape

satin ankle straps offer a bit of shine

In an Orla Kiely skirt and Burberry Prorsum wedges.

the halter style is pretty yet sexy

tweedy fabric adds interesting texture

HALTER DRESS & HEELS
Ashley Madekwe's ruffled skirt and gathered neckline lend a feminine feel to a simple palette.

In a Camilla and Marc dress, Jennifer Behr headband, Karine Sultan cuff and Topshop heels.

a fun, subtle pop of color

In an Eva Mendes for New York & Company coat, dress and necklace.

PINK COAT, DRESS & PUMPS
Eva Mendes's statement necklace brings a touch of sparkle to flowy shapes and a soft palette.

Shop the Feminine Look!

ANN TAYLOR
anntaylor.com
Check out the polished separates, sheath dresses and ladylike statement accessories.

ANTHROPOLOGIE
anthropologie.com
Look no further for pieces with a more laid-back, airy vibe, like breezy blouses and tasseled necklaces.

BANANA REPUBLIC
bananarepublic.com
Get feminine staples like dresses and blouses, plus pretty jewelry perfect for every day.

KATE SPADE NEW YORK
katespade.com
Visit this go-to retailer for the ultimate girlie girl to find full skirts, jewelry with bows and more.

REBECCA TAYLOR
rebeccataylor.com
Shop the printed tops and dresses the brand's known for as well as polished pants and little jackets.

TORY BURCH
toryburch.com
Find sophisticated must-haves from structured handbags to chic dresses.

THE MUST-HAVE PIECES

Create a **girlie look with floaty dresses, pointy pumps** and more—they're your new wardrobe essentials! **Delicate shapes and details** make them so pretty and right on-trend

PEARL STUDS

They add an elegant touch to an outfit, even if they're faux

FLORAL DRESS

A flowery print gives any silhouette—from fit-and-flares to sheaths—a romantic spin

PASTEL COAT

A soft color with ladylike details (think a flippy hem) takes wool outerwear from basic to beyond cute

LOW HEELS

A pointy toe and midi heel are flattering, while a sweet embellishment adds charm

STRUCTURED SATCHEL

A fun color and dainty trim feel sophisticated on a structured carryall

RUFFLE TOP

Flowy ruffles transform any top into a flirty, fashionable go-to

ENVELOPE CLUTCH

A sleek clutch with a ladylike accent is perfect for going out

COLORFUL JEANS

Lavender, powder blue and other light hues offer casual skinnies a delightful twist

T-STRAP HEELS

In brights or neutrals, the retro style is so feminine

COLLAR NECKLACE

A delicate design and jewels enhance a neckline

FULL SKIRT

A voluminous shape and demure knee-length hem are undeniably girlie

More Feminine Must-Haves:

PETER PAN COLLAR TOP

SLIP DRESS

SILKY BLOUSE

SOFT CARDI

BOXY TWEED JACKET

TRUMPET MIDI

EMBELLISHED SWEATER

PEPLUM TOP

POINTY D'ORSAY FLATS

SKINNY BOW BELT

BRACELET WATCH

LACY T-SHIRT

The vintagey feel makes it a dressier substitute for your little cotton tee

7 TRICKS TO GET
A FEMININE LOOK

1

Have fun with hair accessories

"Wear a jeweled barrette, flower or a headband," says celeb stylist Nicole Chavez. It's such an easy—and slightly unexpected—way to incorporate a girlie flair.

2

Play up your lashes and cheeks

"Long lashes feel flirty, so try a lengthening mascara or actual false eyelashes," says Chavez. Take it a step further by sweeping a pinky blush across your cheeks for a natural rosy-looking flush.

3

Create an instant hourglass

"Wear a thick belt with a dress, or tuck a tank into an A-line skirt to really highlight your middle," says Chavez. Make sure you focus on the smallest part of your waist for the most flattering look.

4

Opt for delicate and playful accessories

"Try cute little heart earrings, pearls or lockets," says celeb stylist Micaela Erlanger. Keep them on the smaller, daintier side—anything too big or chunky can overwhelm your style.

Lauren Conrad's sparkles and flowy waves look supersweet.

It's easier than you think **to master a style that's charming yet right on-trend.** Here we share the latest **tips and outfit ideas** from celeb stylists and more

5

Go for pumps

"A pointy or semiround closed toe is timeless and ladylike," says Erlanger. "Avoid a style with a platform." For extra girlishness, try a pretty solid color, like pink, or something with jewels.

6

Add vintagey pieces

"Jewelry with an antique feel, like a slightly tarnished gold necklace or a cocktail ring, has a romantic vibe," says Chavez. Whether they're actually vintage or just look it, cameos, pearls and charm bracelets also fit the bill.

7

Incorporate colors and prints

"Pastel hues like mint green, pale blue and lavender are having a big moment right now," says celeb stylist Ilaria Urbinati. "They're feminine but in a chic way." Patterns like polka dots and florals have a fun feel that's still so stylish.

GET THE LOOK
In shiny patent, a bow belt is the perfect dressy feminine accent, and a cameo necklace gives a charming retro touch.

Sarah Jessica Parker mixes pastels and a floral print for an extra-girlie feel.

In an Alice + Olivia by Stacey Bendet jacket, Giles dress, House of Lavande bracelet and ring and SJP pumps.

STYLE SETTER

LAUREN CONRAD

The clothing designer, author and lifestyle guru works a **sweet, romantic vibe** like no one else. Sticking to a mix of girlie and **ladylike silhouettes—**from fit-and-flares to body-skimming sheaths—her go-to style is flirty and figure-flattering. **Floral prints, polka dots and other playful details** keep it feeling fresh, while **more modern extras,** like top-handle satchels, oversize sunnies and sleek pumps, tie this pretty look together with ease

LACY DRESS

In a Paper Crown dress and Christian Louboutin pumps.

PATTERNED SHEATH

In a Badgley Mischka dress.

BREEZY MAXIDRESS

In a Heartloom dress.

> **"** I love beautiful things like lace, pink and bows. Part of the fun of being a girl is dressing like one!"
> —Lauren Conrad

PRINTED TOP & PASTEL SKIRT

In a Tibi top, Paper Crown skirt, Emmanuelle Khanh sunglasses and Casadei pumps with a Chanel bag.

POLKA DOT LBD & BOW PUMPS

In an LC Lauren Conrad dress and pumps.

COLORFUL FIT-AND-FLARE

In an Alice + Olivia by Stacey Bendet dress.

PRETTY TOP, SKINNIES & FLATS

In Emmanuelle Khanh sunglasses.

FLORAL MINIDRESS

In a Lela Rose dress and Casadei pumps.

365 DAYS OF

Pieces that **add a sweet vibe** will keep you looking good

WINTER

Ladylike pieces make a pretty statement while keeping you warm—think colorful coats, brocade dresses and top-handle bags

Eva
Mendes

Lily
Collins

Alexa
Chung

Elizabeth
Olsen

Zooey
Deschanel

Sarah Jessica
Parker

GREAT STYLE

ear-round! Check out these celebs' seasonal outfits

SPRING

In milder temps, midi skirts, peplums and more—in florals, embellished fabrics and pastels—have a playful vibe

Rosie Huntington-Whiteley

Zoë Saldana

Blake Lively

Emma Stone

Freida Pinto

Angie Harmon

SUMMER

Lightweight minis, flowy skirts and delicate white tops help create romantic, sunny-day outfits

| Olivia Munn | Camilla Belle | Alessandra Ambrosio | Selena Gomez | Brooklyn Decker | Selita Ebanks |

FALL

Dark florals, soft knits and other covered-up finds give the season's style a girlie look

Holland
Roden

Lily
Collins

Kylie
Minogue

Bella
Thorne

Jessica
Alba

Kelly
Rowland

FEMININE LOOKS
THROUGH THE AGES

Style icons including Brigitte Bardot and Sophia Loren **embody this romantic, playful mood.** See why they're proof you can never go wrong with **a ruffled top, floral dress and a well-placed bow**

Catherine Deneuve
1962
The French actress plays up the charming appeal of a satin bow (or two!).

Brigitte Bardot
1970
The screen siren hits the road in a flouncy boho dress and oversize hat.

Whitney Houston
1987
The musical diva's simple knit dress is so flattering in a soft shade of pink.

Jane Birkin
1973
The actress and singer adds a flirty, frilly top to her frayed jeans and platform slingbacks.

Audrey Hepburn
1954
The *Sabrina* leading lady is striking in a floral-strewn strapless gown.

Ava Gardner
1954
In *The Barefoot Contessa*, the silver-screen beauty doesn't underestimate the allure of layered ruffles.

Natalie Wood
1966
The film star is polished and pretty in an embellished sheath and satin flats.

Sophia Loren
1955
The Italian actress works a sweet yet sexy halter dress in a floral print with matching pumps.

Molly Ringwald
1986
In *Pretty in Pink*, the star gives a quirky twist to menswear with pastels and flower details.

Twiggy
1967
In her cotton voile minidress and ballets, the model is the height of girlie.

95

mascara on both top and bottom lashes really plays up eyes

rosy blush enhances cheekbones in a natural-looking way

LOTS OF LASHES & WAVY STRANDS
Kerry Washington highlights her eyes with fluttery lashes and brow-skimming fringe, plus supersoft waves.

CAN'T-MISS
BEAUTY LOOKS

Feminine hair and makeup are all about playing up your girlie side—**lush lashes, rosy cheeks, pink lips** and more. Get inspired by these standout celeb ideas

HIGH BUN & FLUSHED CHEEKS
Holland Roden pairs a topknot with a rosy blush to create a demure vibe.

SIDE BRAID & PINK LIPS
Emma Stone reads youthful with a loosely plaited style and fresh-feeling lip color.

WISPY UPDO
Emilia Clarke looks effortlessly ladylike with a relaxed French twist.

a light purple shadow adds a surprise pop to a daytime look

PASTEL MAKEUP
Rachel Bilson is so sweet with a flirty palette—lavender shadow and pink lips.

SUBTLE MAKEUP
Gugu Mbatha-Raw's natural beauty shines with deep purple shadow and pink lips and cheeks.

PRETTY WAVES
Alexa Chung gets her textured look right—a high-shine finish and softness make it feel special.

BRAIDED UPDO
Bella Thorne pulls off a romantic vibe by weaving a ribbon into her braid.

The Tool Kit
Your must-haves to get feminine right— lipstick, shadow, nail polish and more

PINK LIPSTICK
Great for day or night, it adds pretty color to lips.

PASTEL SHADOW
Shades like lilac, baby blue and even mint green are softer ways to wear color.

CURLING MASCARA
It gives lashes definition with the bonus of a flattering bend.

ROSY BLUSH
Pink tones give cheeks healthy color—as if you actually blushed.

GLITTER NAIL POLISH
A little sparkle makes nails feel playful.

GLAM

Some pieces always make a statement: **sparkly dresses, bold jewelry, stilettos.** Whether you dress them up or down, they're **completely eye-catching.** Sound like your kind of look? Here's everything you need to know to channel this vibe—and give it a fresh, modern feel

10 CAN'T-MISS **GLAM** LOOKS

Stylish celebs like Elle Macpherson, Rita Ora and Blake Lively show **the newest ways to wear luxe, notice-me pieces.** See how they work it for day and night, and get inspired to tweak—or totally transform—your own look!

gold bracelets add instant drama

SLOUCHY TOP & METALLIC SKINNIES
Elle Macpherson makes casual silhouettes extra-special with shots of bold silver and gold.

a slim, ankle-length cut keeps the look in proportion

superhigh studded stilettos kick the vibe up a notch

In a Topshop sweater, Balmain pants and Christian Louboutin heels with an Alexander McQueen clutch.

GLITTERY MINIDRESS **Carrie Underwood's** look is all about sparkle, but her dress's easy shape keeps it from feeling like too much.

long sleeves give a minidress a sophisticated spin

a structured clutch creates contrast with the flowy dress

gemstone-encrusted sandals add an extra dose of luxe

In a Badgley Mischka dress and Jimmy Choo heels with a Jimmy Choo clutch.

a blazer
worn without
a blouse =
so sexy

**METALLIC
TUXEDO**
Ashley Madekwe's
menswear-inspired bronze
suit is a modern way to
wear metallics and
needs just minimal
accessories.

tailored shorts
show some
leg but still feel
elegant

a frame clutch
offers a
ladylike touch

In Christian
Louboutin
heels with
a Giuseppe
Zanotti
Design clutch.

a matching belt gives the dress shape

In an Emilio Pucci dress, Lorraine Schwartz earrings, a Jennifer Fisher necklace and Jimmy Choo heels.

In a vintage dress.

GOWN & STRAPPY HEELS
Rita Ora's long-sleeve dress is unexpectedly sexy with sequins, a plunging neckline and thigh-high slit.

LEOPARD-PRINT MINIDRESS & BLACK PUMPS
Joy Bryant lets a bold, body-hugging style shine with simple heels and subtle jewelry.

FURRY-COLLAR COAT & LEATHER SKINNIES

Cat Deeley makes a statement coat feel chic by pairing it with an unbuttoned blouse and fitted leather pants.

a fluffy collar in bright pink is so fun

a gold necklace creates dimension

In a Matthew Williamson coat and top and Jimmy Choo heels with a Chanel clutch.

glittery accents mean no necklace required

SILKY DRESS & POINTY PUMPS

Blake Lively opts for flirty styles made extra-special with dressy details and touches of sparkle.

the ruffled hem is ultra-feminine

In a Jenny Packham dress, Lorraine Schwartz ring and Christian Louboutin heels.

a cool take on gold hoops

with furry details and studs, it has that total wow factor

PLUSH VEST & PATTERNED JEANS
Heidi Klum creates a rich mix of textures, but in a subdued palette they're eye-catching, not over-the-top.

the pattern is subtle yet looks so luxe

In a Thomas Wylde vest, Current/ Elliott jeans and Christian Louboutin heels.

SEQUIN DRESS
Gabrielle Union's embellished sheath is sophisticated and glam in a darker hue with peep-toe heels.

allover sequins bring a strapless style from simple to standout

sleek heels let the dress take center stage

In a Dolce & Gabbana dress, Kara Ackerman earrings and Giuseppe Zanotti Design heels.

In a Skaist Taylor coat, Paul & Joe Sister top, Bebe pants and Christian Louboutin heels with a Proenza Schouler clutch.

FURRY COAT & TROUSERS
Kourtney Kardashian takes tailored pants up a notch with a dramatic topper and snake-print heels.

Shop the Glam Look!

BCBG MAX AZRIA
bcbg.com
Find fun night-out dresses, silky strappy tops and gorgeous statement accessories.

BAUBLE BAR
baublebar.com
Shop the glam girls' essentials: statement jewelry—from blingy necklaces to jewel-encrusted ear cuffs!

BEBE *bebe.com*
Check out sexy, affordably priced pieces, including body-con dresses, drapey tops and sky-high stilettos.

JUSTFAB *justfab.com*
Get an eye-catching look for less with this site's knockout heels, little dresses and going-out bags.

MICHAEL KORS
michaelkors.com
Channel a jet-set vibe with the brand's furry vests, luxe knits, oversize sunnies, "it" bags and more.

VINCE CAMUTO
vincecamuto.com
Don't miss this one-stop shop for glam must-haves like animal-print dresses, faux leather skinnies and (of course) fab shoes.

THE MUST-HAVE PIECES

Go for a **sexy vibe with showstopping dresses, heeled booties** and more—they're your new wardrobe essentials! **Bold hues and pops of rich texture** make them so special and right on-trend

SEQUIN DRESS

You can't go wrong with a little sparkle—it's the perfect option for a night out

LEOPARD-PRINT BOOTIES

The go-to pattern makes an instant statement on high-heel booties

FURRY VEST

Over a sweater or blouse, it's a superluxe layering piece

GOLD HOOPS

An oversize style is so easy to wear—and has a wow factor

PLUSH SCARF

It adds luxurious texture to whatever you're wearing

DRAPEY SKIRT

Shorter lengths and drapey or shiny fabrics make for a flirty look

STRAPPY STILETTOS

Paired with a red pedi, they're total outfit-makers

OVERSIZE SHADES

Dramatic round frames have a movie-star vibe

JEWELED BANGLE

A gorgeous extra is all you need to lend a fierce accent to any look

METALLIC JEANS

The closet staple gets a major boost in metallic— just pair with a white tee and go

More Glam Must-Haves:

BODY-CON DRESS

COCKTAIL RING

PLATFORM HEELS

SPARKLY CLUTCH

ANIMAL-PRINT COAT

WEDGE SNEAKERS

TO-THE-KNEE BOOTS

MOHAIR SWEATER

BEJEWELED NECKLACE

GOLD BANGLES

SILKY JUMPSUIT

EMBELLISHED BAG

Shiny hardware takes a can't-miss carryall up a notch

7 TRICKS TO GET
A GLAM LOOK

1

Go sexy but sophisticated

"Your clothes don't all need to be body-con, but they should show off your best assets," say celeb stylists Rob Zangardi and Mariel Haenn. To keep it refined, choose one area to play up at a time, whether it's your legs in a micromini or your décolletage in a plunging neckline.

2

Pay attention to the shoes

"They can make or break an outfit," says celeb stylist Mel Ottenberg. "I always look for a stiletto heel as high as it can go." Other details to consider are sparkly embellishments and fun straps.

3

Choose dramatic hair and makeup

"A deep side part gives a nod to Old Hollywood glamour and adds an air of mystery," say Zangardi and Haenn. For your face, try the knockout combo of a red lip paired with a smoky eye.

4

Be tastefully over-the-top

"Offset your most glam pieces with simpler styles," say Zangardi and Haenn. "It will keep you from looking like you're trying too hard." Balance an eye-catching coat or vest with basic skinnies and clean pumps or an allover sequin dress with sleek, neutral extras.

Eva Longoria's faux feather vest and platforms luxe up basics.

In a Sabine vest and Christian Louboutin boots.

It's easier than you think **to master a style that's luxurious yet so fun.** Here we share the latest **tips and outfit ideas** from celeb stylists and more

5

Add metallics

"Silver or gold pumps are as easy to wear as neutral ones," say Zangardi and Haenn. "And they add a little hint of shine." Coated skinnies or a shimmery jacket are other ways to rock the trend.

6

Pile on the jewelry

"Layer rings and bracelets or go for a bold necklace with lots of rhinestones," says celeb stylist Jen Rade. Loads of bling is one of the easiest ways to take a simple outfit and turn it into a statement-maker.

7

Opt for anything red

"It's hard to wear red without standing out," say Zangardi and Haenn. And standing out is your goal! Go bold in a red body-con dress or wear just a pop of the color on heels or a clutch.

GET THE LOOK
Even in a trendy mini size, a leopard-print clutch with hardware looks rich, and sparkly bracelets give any outfit a notice-me touch.

Miranda Kerr's red dress in a curve-skimming fit is so striking.

In a Roland Mouret dress and a Cartier bracelet.

STYLE SETTER
JENNIFER LOPEZ

The supersultry performer never fails to deliver a **showstopping look.** In body-con dresses, miniskirts, **sexy rompers and more,** she always makes a major statement—and with tons of confidence! **Sequins, furry accents and animal prints** add an ultraglitzy feel, while **notice-me finishing touches—**everything from strappy stilettos to standout bags to over-the-knee boots—give each outfit that signature wow factor

NEON
ROMPER

In a Jennifer Lopez for Kohl's
romper, Givenchy necklaces
and Ivy Kirzhner heels.

FURRY-COLLAR
COAT &
PEEP-TOE
HEELS

In a Diane von Furstenberg coat,
Givenchy dress and
Giuseppe Zanotti Design heels
with a Valentino clutch.

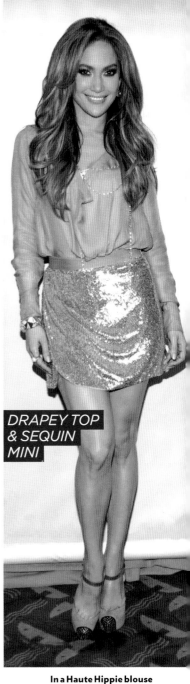

DRAPEY TOP
& SEQUIN
MINI

In a Haute Hippie blouse
and skirt and Christian
Louboutin heels.

66

Jennifer mixes bold pieces with a timeless femininity, and she isn't afraid of a little sparkle—or a lot of it."
—Rob Zangardi & Mariel Haenn, Jennifer's stylists

GLITTERY DRESS

LUXE SCARF & LACE-UP BOOTIES

In a KaufmanFranco dress and Jimmy Choo heels with a Jimmy Choo clutch.

In The Row pants, Dita sunglasses, Gucci scarf and Christian Dior booties with a Fendi bag.

BODYSUIT & PANTS

In a Gucci bodysuit
and pants and Giuseppe
Zanotti Design heels.

LEOPARD-PRINT JACKET & MINI

In an A.L.C. jacket and skirt and
Christian Louboutin boots.

EMBELLISHED MINIDRESS

In a Zuhair Murad dress
and Christian Louboutin heels
with a Kotur clutch.

365 DAYS OF

Pieces that **make a luxe statement** will keep you looking good

WINTER

Leather skinnies, major coats and slinky dresses are showstopping—
fur, fringe and sequins add glitz

| Carrie Underwood | Kate Moss | Kelly Rowland | Nicole Richie | Jennifer Lopez | Alessandra Ambrosio |

GREAT STYLE

year-round! Check out these celebs' seasonal outfits

Iridescent fabrics, metallic beading and more feel special on everything from sheath dresses to strappy sandals

Malin
Akerman

Olivia
Palermo

Kourtney
Kardashian

Ciara

Kylie
Minogue

Jessica
Biel

SUMMER

**Jumpsuits, shorts and dresses look supersexy for rising temps
in trendy prints and solid white**

Olivia
Palermo

Elle
Macpherson

Selita
Ebanks

Emmy
Rossum

Sofia
Vergara

Gabrielle
Union

Autumnal layers, like plush vests and notice-me scarves, create comfy, sophisticated looks that are total standouts

Kate
Hudson

Cat
Deeley

Olivia
Palermo

Elle
Macpherson

Kim
Kardashian

Kylie
Minogue

GLAM LOOKS
THROUGH THE AGES

Style icons including Marilyn Monroe and Elizabeth Taylor **embody this sultry, glitzy mood.** See why they're proof you can never go wrong with **a satin dress and a touch of fur or feathers**

Diana Ross
1974
The music diva's gorgeous makeup, jewels and fur give off a dramatic vibe.

Josephine Baker
1925
The iconic singer makes a satin wrap extra luxe with an extravagant collar.

Marilyn Monroe
1953
The film legend works her *Gentlemen Prefer Blondes* pleated halter gown.

Elizabeth Hurley
1994
The Brit actress and model takes a daring step in her cutout dress.

Rita Hayworth
1946
The thigh-high slit adds a supersexy touch to the star's strapless gown in *Gilda*.

Veronica Lake
1941
The silver-screen goddess is stunning with platinum waves and a dark lip in *I Wanted Wings*.

Elizabeth Taylor
1950s
The actress's shirred dress and dazzling earrings are knockouts.

Lauren Bacall
1944
The leading lady uses zebra print to amp up a sleek pencil skirt.

Jean Harlow
1933
In *Dinner at Eight*, the star artfully mixes glitter with a boa and a touch of lace.

Joan Collins
1985
The *Dynasty* actress's character wraps herself in attention-grabbing glitz.

SMOKY EYES & TOUSLED WAVES
Beyoncé looks extra-sultry with metallic shadow and glossy pink lips, plus a high-volume, textured do.

neutral lips bring all of the attention to the eyes

CAN'T-MISS
BEAUTY LOOKS

Glam hair and makeup are all about going for it in a notice-me way—**sexy waves, a gorgeous updo, smoky eyes** and more. Get inspired by these standout celeb ideas

SWEPT-BACK STRANDS
Kate Upton rocks a going-out look—a smooth do pulled back on one side, plus striking red lips.

HALF-UP DO
Jennifer Lopez's '60s-inspired, voluminous hairstyle is sheer retro glam.

FRENCH TWIST
Lea Michele's stylish updo gets a kittenish touch with long sideswept bangs.

starting
waves at
the jawline
feels soft
and easy

ORANGE LIPS & CASCADING WAVES

Jessica Alba is stunning with a vibrant lipstick and glossy hair ever so elegantly swept over one shoulder.

LONG, SHINY STRANDS
Sofia Vergara is sexy with flowing waves that have touchable volume.

BOLD MAKEUP & PIXIE
Jennifer Lawrence balances intense color on both her eyes and lips with a playful cropped cut.

ULTRASMOKY EYES
Jennifer Hudson plays up her eyes with dark winged-out shadow.

The Tool Kit
Your must-haves to get glam right—lipstick, shadow, nail polish and more

SMOKY EYE SHADOW
Dark shadows—black, gunmetal, brown—work on everyone.

FALSE EYELASHES
More dramatic than just mascara, they add extra flirtiness.

HIGHLIGHTER
It gives every skin tone a gorgeous glow.

METALLIC NAIL POLISH
Shimmery shades like gold, pewter and bronze instantly add glitz to nails.

NUDE LIPSTICK
A skin-tone flattering shade is so versatile.

RED LIPSTICK
It's the quintessential go-to color for statement-making lips.

OOL

Some pieces just say tough-chic: **moto jackets, leather skinnies, anything black.** Whether you dress them up or down, they're **always on-trend.** Sound like your kind of look? Here's everything you need to know to channel this vibe—and give it a fresh, modern feel

10 CAN'T-MISS **COOL** LOOKS

Stylish celebs like Alessandra Ambrosio, Gwen Stefani and Ciara show **the newest ways to wear edgy, effortless pieces.** See how they work it for day and night, and get inspired to tweak—or totally transform—your own look!

delicate layered necklaces create contrast

two-tone skinnies offer a graphic look

hardware gives heeled ankle boots a rock-and-roll vibe

In an Anine Bing jacket, Hudson Jeans jeans and Christian Louboutin boots.

MOTO JACKET & SKINNIES
Alessandra Ambrosio gives tough leather and denim pieces a chic twist with fitted silhouettes.

gold and
white stripes
are an
unexpected
and fun
touch

a relaxed
style has an
easy feel

**TANK &
SLOUCHY
JEANS**
Gwen Stefani's black
extras keep her printed
boyfriends looking
fashion-forward and
not over-the-top.

peep-toes
are a sexy
take on a
black bootie

In Maison
Martin
Margiela
booties.

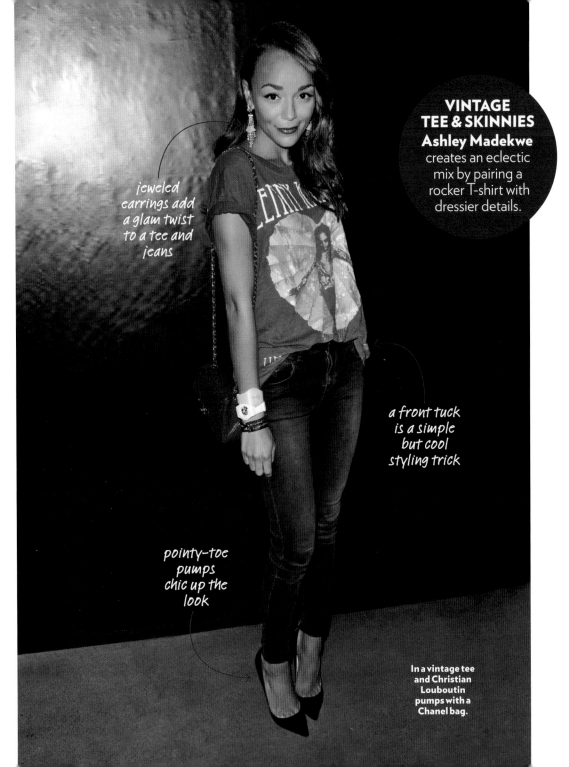

VINTAGE TEE & SKINNIES
Ashley Madekwe creates an eclectic mix by pairing a rocker T-shirt with dressier details.

jeweled earrings add a glam twist to a tee and jeans

a front tuck is a simple but cool styling trick

pointy-toe pumps chic up the look

In a vintage tee and Christian Louboutin pumps with a Chanel bag.

blue is a fun alternative to black

BRIGHT JACKET & BOYFRIENDS
Kelly Rowland's unfussy combo feels fresh with shots of eye-catching color and metallics.

In an Acne Studios jacket.

ankle-strap heels in gleaming silver stand out

In an American Apparel top, Topshop pants and Givenchy heels.

MOTO JACKET & LEGGINGS
Miley Cyrus's studded jacket lends an edgy feel to her crop top and plaid bottoms.

HEAD-TO-TOE BLACK
Jessica Biel's moto jacket, wide belt, chain-strap bag and aviators add interest to her monochromatic look.

a quilted bag adds a polished contrast to edgier pieces

a thick leather belt toughens up a flowy dress

the mix of materials lends a trendy touch

In an Azzedine Alaïa belt and AllSaints boots with a Chanel bag.

a metallic bib necklace amps up the outfit

ARMY JACKET & LEATHER DRESS
Sophia Bush creates a modern look, pairing a casual military jacket with a sleek fit-and-flare silhouette and trendy accessories.

the animal-print clutch is a glam touch

a short, flippy dress in leather adds a flirt factor

In a Reformation jacket, A.L.C. dress, Dannijo necklace and Chloé boots with a Clare Vivier clutch.

the hat and sunglasses lend an effortlessly cool vibe

leathery sleeves take a sporty jacket up a notch

VARSITY JACKET & SKINNIES
Ciara gives her black outfit a tomboyish spin with an athletic-inspired jacket and knit beanie.

lace-up platforms are a sexy addition

In a Joyrich jacket.

vertical ribbing elongates the body

a menswear watch makes a statement

DRESS & HIGH-TOPS
Rita Ora's chunky sneakers add a sporty pop to a maxidress.

In an Adidas Originals x Opening Ceremony dress.

in black and white, they go with everything

In a Maje coat, Citizens of Humanity jeans and a Reason Clothing hat.

JACKET, SKINNIES & SNEAKS
Cara Delevingne's streamlined jacket adds instant polish to an otherwise laid-back outfit.

Shop the Cool Look!

DKNY
dkny.com
Find on-trend dresses, bags, jackets and more that have a sexy, urban look and are inspired by New York City.

NASTY GAL
nastygal.com
Visit this online shop for looks that range from edgy to daring—think vintage tees, supershort cutoffs and quirky-print jumpsuits.

RAG & BONE
rag-bone.com
Check out this celeb-fave brand for motorcycle booties, leather jackets and more—it's the epitome of downtown cool.

REBECCA MINKOFF
rebeccaminkoff.com
Shop this hot designer's clothing and accessories with tough-chic details like studs and cutouts.

RIVER ISLAND
riverisland.com
Get **wardrobe** essentials that have an **outside-the-**box twist from cool bomber jackets to chunky wedges.

TOPSHOP
topshop.com
Stock up on standouts like printed dresses and chunky jewelry, as well as pieces from collabs with celebs like Kate Moss.

SNEAKERS

In a solid hue or allover print, laid-back kicks offer outfits a trendy twist

THE
MUST-
HAVE
PIECES

Rock an **edgy vibe with leather jackets, moto boots** and more—they're your new wardrobe essentials! **Fashion-forward details like studs and chains** make them so daring and right on-trend

MOTORCYCLE JACKET

A total go-to, it can be worn with anything from a dress to skinnies

RING PARTY

Stacking unexpected styles, mixing metals and more create a cutting-edge look

EDGY HEELS

Day or night, high heels with straps, hardware and cutouts are rocker chic

MINISKIRT

In punk-inspired fabrics and prints like leather and plaid, a short hemline has a cool-girl feel

LEATHER LEGGINGS

Real or faux, they're superhot— and so luxe

BOLD NECKLACE

A statement necklace gets tough with chains or spikes

CÉLFIE

GRAPHIC TEE

A little attitude— clever sayings, logos and more— takes your T-shirt game up a notch

MOTO BOOTS

Whether sleek or chunky, simple or embellished, they're perfect for every day

STUDDED BAG

Metal detailing turns a simple black purse into a downtown staple

CAMO PRINT

The hip pattern adds a bold touch to any look—from sweaters to skinnies

More Cool Must-Haves:

CHOKER NECKLACE

LOOSE-WEAVE SWEATER

EAR CUFF

LEATHER PENCIL SKIRT

ROCKER TEE

BLACK SKINNIES

AVIATOR SUNGLASSES

STUDDED PUMPS

FLANNEL BUTTON-UP

LEATHER CUFF BRACELET

BOYFRIEND JEANS

With heels or booties, the slouchy style is a closet essential

7 TRICKS TO GET
A COOL LOOK

1

Experiment with fashion-forward silhouettes

"Crop tops and sweatshirts have an of-the-moment feel," say celeb stylists Rob Zangardi and Mariel Haenn. Another big trend: denim overalls. "Wear them with something cropped underneath and heels to give them a sexy spin," says celeb stylist Nicole Chavez.

2

Include a surprising touch

"Something with '70s flair, like fringe, feels big now," say Zangardi and Haenn. "Just keep it sleek." Or try a head scarf or body jewelry to really up the cool factor.

3

Add interest with cool fabrics

"Look for materials with interesting textures, like neoprene and mesh," says Chavez. Not only are they in style, but they'll make even the most simple pieces—T-shirts, minis and more—stand out.

4

Go for statement-making jewelry

"Earrings in general are having a major moment," says Kate Dimmock, STYLEWATCH fashion director. "Nothing says 'fashion risk-taker' quite like an ear cuff." Other ways to have fun with jewelry: Mix and match studs for day or wear just one dangling earring for a night out.

Kate Bosworth's sweatshirt and sheer maxi-skirt pairing feels so fresh. **In an H&M skirt and Cutler and Gross sunglasses.**

It's easier than you think **to master a style that's trendy and fun yet totally unique.** Here we share the latest **tips and outfit ideas** from celeb stylists and more

5

Choose unexpected shoes

"Casual shoes have now been elevated to high fashion," says Chavez. While sporting sneakers is the easiest way to work the trend, try '90s favorites like creepers and high-top Dr. Martens.

6

Make your mani stand out

"I love the idea of nail polish in a gunmetal gray or silver," says Chavez. "Think of it as the new alternative to black or dark purple." Nail art and pointed tips also feel true to the tough-chic vibe.

7

Mix contrasting vibes

"**Try wearing trainers or a rocker tee with a chic skirt, or boyfriends with a crisp, white men's shirt and your strappiest heels,**" say Zangardi and Haenn. **The surprising combos will give your look that offhand touch.**

GET THE LOOK
Sneakers are so right-now, and ear cuffs add a daring twist to any look.

Olivia Wilde's vintage rocker tee and sleek skirt create unexpected contrast. **In a vintage tee, Robert Rodriguez skirt, Cresta Bledsoe cuff and Jimmy Choo pumps with a Smythson clutch.**

STYLE SETTER
RIHANNA

The chart-topping singer and pop-culture icon is a **fashion risk-taker** who totally owns it! In distressed denim, midriff-baring tops and body-hugging dresses, her outfits are unexpected and **always ahead of the curve.** A simple palette keeps her looks from appearing over-the-top, while **cool add-ons** like tomboyish baseball jackets, **sexy heels and chunky jewelry** create a modern mix that makes a statement every time

DENIM BUTTON-UP & DISTRESSED PENCIL SKIRT

In a Current/Elliott shirt, Acne Studios skirt and Manolo Blahnik pumps with a Juliette Jake clutch.

LWD & HIGH-TOPS

In an A.L.C. dress and Converse sneakers.

CAMO PULLOVER & DARK DENIM

In a Rihanna for River Island top, jeans and heels and Le Specs sunglasses with a Givenchy clutch.

> " Rihanna's style comes from her confidence– she's a natural rebel who wants to set the trends, not follow them."
> —Mel Ottenberg, Rihanna's stylist

HOLOGRAM TOP & RIPPED BOYFRIENDS

CROP TOP & SWEAT PANTS

In a Stella McCartney top, Acne Studios jeans and Manolo Blahnik heels with a Stella McCartney clutch.

In Isaora pants, Trapstar jacket, House of Holland sunglasses and Manolo Blahnik heels.

BASEBALL JACKET, MIDI & SNEAKS

In a Fay jacket and
New Balance sneakers.

OVERALLS & LACE-UP HEELS

In Topshop overalls, Silver Spoon
Attire hat, Chanel necklace
and cuff and Sophia Webster heels
with a Givenchy bag.

VARSITY JACKET, MESH TOP & SKINNIES

In a Rihanna for River Island
jacket, top, jeans, jewelry,
belt and heels.

365 DAYS OF

Pieces that **create a tough-chic mix** will keep you looking goo

Standout layers, black leather and bold outerwear ward off the cold while making a statement

| Jamie Chung | Gwen Stefani | Jessica Alba | Rita Ora | Rachel Bilson | Nicky Hilton |

GREAT STYLE

year-round! Check out these celebs' seasonal outfits

SPRING

Ripped boyfriend jeans, graphic tees, mini cross-body bags and more lighten up a look but still feel edgy

Olivia   Ashley   Kate   Rita   Kate   Cara
Munn   Madekwe   Mara   Ora   Bosworth   Delevingne

SUMMER

Everything from tank tops and leather leggings to cage sandals and short shorts give warm-weather looks a rocker vibe

| Nicole Richie | Kendall Jenner | Miley Cyrus | Jamie Chung | Gwen Stefani | Solange Knowles |

An eclectic mix—think a moto jacket and sweatpants or a chunky sweater with a leather zippered skirt—is cozy yet unexpected

| Shay Mitchell | Ciara | Gwen Stefani | Alexa Chung | Keira Knightley | Selena Gomez |

COOL LOOKS THROUGH THE AGES

Style icons including Madonna and Debbie Harry **embody this edgy, risk-taking mood.** See why they're proof you can never go wrong with **rocker tees, leather pants and serious boots**

Debbie Harry
1977
·············
The Blondie babe steps out in high-waisted camo pants and a tough moto.

Jane Fonda
1971
·············
The actress works a miniskirt and over-the-knee boots in *Klute*.

Lisa Bonet
1986
·············
The TV star mixes artsy black and white pieces in a daring way.

Chrissie Hynde
1980
·············
The Pretenders legend rocks out in an ironic T-shirt, leather pants and tousled hair.

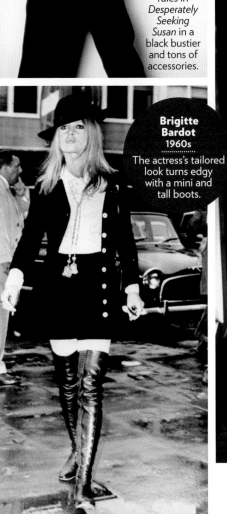

Madonna
1985
....
The queen of pop totally rules in *Desperately Seeking Susan* in a black bustier and tons of accessories.

Brigitte Bardot
1960s
....
The actress's tailored look turns edgy with a mini and tall boots.

Françoise Hardy
1960s
....
The French chanteuse goes for a mod street-style look with a belted two-tone ensemble and white ankle boots.

Cher
1960s
....
The pop star sports an all-white jacket and trousers with funky printed boots.

Pat Benatar
1980
....
The singer sounds off in a fitted striped tee, tight leather skinnies and heeled booties.

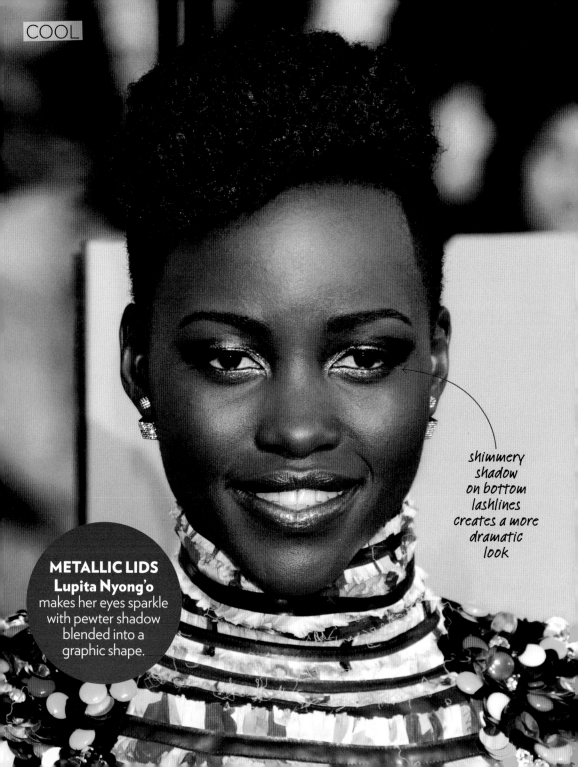

shimmery
shadow
on bottom
lashlines
creates a more
dramatic
look

METALLIC LIDS
Lupita Nyong'o
makes her eyes sparkle
with pewter shadow
blended into a
graphic shape.

CAN'T-MISS
BEAUTY LOOKS

Cool hair and makeup are all about adding edge—**a trendy updo, unexpected hair color, graphic eye makeup** and more. Get inspired by these standout celeb ideas

PIECEY CROP
Miley Cyrus adds a playful touch to her short do by spiking it up into a faux-hawk.

SIDE-SHAVEN STYLE & RED LIPS
Rihanna screams cool with a style that's buzzed on one side plus bright matte lips.

PURPLE HAIR
Nicole Richie makes a colorful statement by pulling up her violet locks into a swirled updo.

*black liner
intensifies
bold shadow
even more*

**PLUM
SHADOW**
Kristen Stewart
channels a rock-and-roll
vibe with rust-colored
lids—it's a sexy and fun
take on a traditional
smoky eye.

UNDONE TEXTURE
Chloë Grace Moretz creates a laid-back look with a style that's mussed up—in a good way.

SMOKY EYE & VOLUMINOUS CURLS
Solange Knowles dazzles with a sky-high Afro plus dark shadow and liner.

WAVY BOB
Rita Ora makes the classic cut feel so-of-the-moment by adding easy texture and height on top.

The Tool Kit
Your must-haves to get cool right—lipstick, shadow, nail polish and more

MATTE RED LIPSTICK
A nonshiny finish makes red feel fresh.

BLACK EYELINER
It adds extra edge to any look.

SMOKY EYE SHADOWS
From black to gray to sliver, rich shades make eyes supersultry.

BLACK SPARKLE NAIL POLISH
A dark shade with metallic flecks makes for a cool mani.

NUDE LIPSTICK
A subtle lip color can be paired with anything.

MORE
INSPIR

ATION

Some outfits aren't about a single vibe, they're just effortlessly fashionable: a tuxedo jacket and skirt, a statement coat and denim skinnies, a simple sheath with playful details. Here, see how **our fave celeb style setters get it right**

MORE CAN'T-MISS LOOKS

Stylish celebs like Blake Lively, Kerry Washington and Emma Stone show **the newest ways to create the perfect outfit.** See how they mix it together (separates, extras, heels), and get inspired to tweak—or totally transform—your own look!

a graphic oversize necklace offers a daring twist

peekaboo sleeves are an unexpected way to show some skin

BLOUSE & TUXEDO PANTS
Blake Lively makes slouchy separates chic by sticking to a black-and-white palette and luxe accessories.

the white tux stripe gives black pants a modern touch

In a Lanvin top, pants and necklace and Gucci heels with a Lanvin clutch.

163

in black,
a hat has a
sophisticated
charm

long sleeves
balance a
midriff-baring
crop top

CROP TOP & VIBRANT HEELS

Beyoncé creates a notice-me mix with graphic stripes and a pop of orange.

a classic pointy-
toe shape keeps
bright heels
from feeling
over-the-top

In a Topshop
top and skirt,
Karen Walker
sunglasses
and Manolo
Blahnik pumps.

an oversize style is comfy and chic

head-to-toe black is always sleek

pushed up sleeves show off an arm party

BOXY TOPS & KITTEN HEELS
Ashley & Mary-Kate Olsen are in perfect proportion, balancing a chunky sweater with skinnies and a cropped jacket with high-waisted pants.

In a Bik Bok by Mary-Kate & Ashley Olsen sweater and jeans and Manolo Blahnik heels.

In Manolo Blahnik heels.

COLLARED DRESS & STRAPPY HEELS
Emma Stone pairs a preppy-chic dress with glam heels for a quirky, cute mix.

a sleek, white buttonless style creates contrast against a bold flirty hem

matching lipstick to a skirt is an unexpected way to pull together an outfit

studs add interest to neutral heels

In a Valentino dress and heels.

In a Stella McCartney dress and Christian Louboutin pumps.

EMBELLISHED DRESS & GLITTERY HEELS

Kerry Washington's playful appliqués make a sophisticated sheath and stilettos fun.

SWEATER, MINISKIRT & HEELS

Rashida Jones's slouchy knit and simple skirt take a fun turn with bold ankle-strap heels and a unique printed clutch.

In a Thakoon sweater and skirt.

an oversize
necklace
lends instant
drama

**SIMPLE TOP
& MIDI SKIRT**
Jaime King makes
boho look fashionable
with of-the-moment
silhouettes and cool
extras.

the combination
of textures
adds interest

a lace-up ballet-
inspired style
keeps platforms
sophisticated

In a Dior top,
skirt, necklace
and heels with
a Dior clutch.

LACE SHIRT & SKIRT
Camilla Belle gives the sweet fabric a sexy spin with see-through bits, while leather accents add edge.

In a Monique Lhuillier top, skirt and belt and Jimmy Choo pumps with a Jimmy Choo clutch.

NEUTRAL SEPARATES & SCARF
Elle Macpherson adds texture with suede and denim while the scarf offers a chic, offhand touch.

In a Banjo & Matilda sweater, Ray-Ban sunglasses and Ash booties.

when worn without a shirt, a menswear-inspired jacket looks modern

TUXEDO JACKET & MINISKIRT
Solange Knowles creates eye-catching contrast pairing a bold blazer with a printed skirt and neutral heels.

the flippy silhouette feels flirty

In a 3.1 Phillip Lim for Target blazer and skirt and Givenchy heels.

In an Acne Studios sweater, Citizens of Humanity jeans, Balmain necklace and Christian Louboutin heels.

SWEATER, JEANS & CHAIN-LINK NECKLACE
Rosie Huntington-Whiteley takes a casual outfit up a notch with glam extras and heels for a night-out look.

TRENCH, SKINNIES & BOOTIES
Kate Bosworth amps up a classic jeans outfit with a silky trench and statement shoes.

In a Burberry trench and Rodarte shoes.

a matching dark bag-and-shoe combo pops against neutrals

whether real or faux, leather glams up a pleated skirt

CABLE-KNIT SWEATER, PLEATED SKIRT & KITTEN HEELS
Alexa Chung makes preppy staples look evening-ready with luxe fabrics and accessories.

In a Madewell sweater, J.W. Anderson x Topshop skirt and Christian Louboutin heels with a Mulberry bag.

bows add extra charm

172

a southwestern pattern looks rustic yet cool

SWEATER COAT & SKINNIES
Cat Deeley puts together a stylish cold-weather look by pairing a long cardigan with sleek leather skinnies in an unexpected shade.

buckles are both edgy and luxe

In Céline sunglasses with a Mulberry bag.

PLAID TOP & PANTS
Ashley Madekwe's structured separates make an otherwise classic print feel modern.

wear the pieces together or on their own

a great alternative to black or nude

In a Topshop shirt and pants and Jimmy Choo pumps.

STATEMENT COAT, SKINNIES & CLUTCH
Olivia Palermo luxes up denim with a bold embroidered coat and embellished extras.

In a Marchesa coat, Le Métier de Beauté necklace and Stuart Weitzman pumps with a Marchesa clutch.

In an Unconditional blazer, Rag & Bone sweater, shirt and jeans and Nicholas Kirkwood pumps with a Rag & Bone bag.

COLORFUL BLAZER, BOYFRIENDS & PUMPS
Karolina Kurkova updates a classic mix with bright color and patterned heels.

the center part is a stylish accent

FISHTAIL BRAID
Nina Dobrev makes her trendy plait feel more sophisticated by keeping the front sleek.

MORE CAN'T-MISS
BEAUTY LOOKS

These hair and makeup ideas—**from great-looking accessories to fun lip colors—**will inspire you to try something new, no matter what vibe you're going for

PURPLE LIPS & LINED EYES
Lupita Nyong'o looks both playful and sexy with a bright lip color and dark eyeliner.

BOUNCY WAVES & ORANGE LIPS
Olivia Munn makes retro new with refined texture, a sparkly hairpin and a right-now lip color.

POMPADOUR MEETS FAUX-HAWK
Julianne Hough gives her updo a modern spin by fluffing the top and pinning up the back.

a cool accessory adds contrast to soft texture

BEDAZZLED BAND
Michelle Williams does pretty with an edge by accessorizing her sideswept crop with a rhinestone-encrusted headband.

TOUSLED WAVES
Blake Lively's undone-and-voluminous texture adds effortlessness to her dressed-up look.

BRAIDED MOHAWK
Selena Gomez's statement-making plaited style is as unique as it is gorgeous.

PINNED DO
Maggie Grace makes bobbies look superstylish by crisscrossing them.

GRAPHIC EYELINER
Sophia Bush artfully accentuates her eyes by creating a cool shape with her black liner.

FRESH HAIR & MAKEUP
Dianna Agron goes for softness all around—pastel shadow and lip color paired with a trendy wavy bob.

LINED EYES & PONY
Jamie Chung balances dark, sultry eye makeup with a fresh-looking low ponytail.

13 CAN'T-MISS **BLOGGER** LOOKS

How do street-style stars pull off their best looks? It's all about **reworking basics in new ways, mixing prints and adding unexpected finishing touches.** Here's all the trendsetting inspiration you need to transform your own outfits

CROPPED LACE TOP & FULL SKIRT

Aimee Song (Song of Style) balances pink hues with delicate black accessories for a bold yet polished statement.

In a Toujouri top and skirt.

In a Tommy Hilfiger blazer, blouse and shorts and Christian Louboutin pumps with a Givenchy bag.

In a J.Crew coat and Christian Louboutin pumps with a Saint Laurent by Hedi Slimane bag.

In a Derek Lam 10 Crosby shirt and Jimmy Choo pumps.

TAILORED SHORT SUIT & STRIPED BLOUSE
Julia Engel (Gal Meets Glam) gives a trendy suit a refined feel with a silky bow-neck shirt and sleek extras.

MILITARY-INSPIRED COAT, SKINNIES & HEELS
Helena Glazer's (Brooklyn Blonde) cuffed red jeans and copper pumps pop against neutral classics.

COLORBLOCK BUTTON-UP & JEANS
Claire Sulmers (The Bomb Life) pairs different shades of blue for a cool tonal look.

In a Boohoo bodysuit and skirt and Guess heels.

V-NECK BODYSUIT, FLIPPY SKIRT & PUMPS
Nadia Aboulhosn (Nadia Aboulhosn) works flirty shapes in solid hues for a feminine look.

PATTERNED DRESS & SNEAKERS
Chiara Ferragni (The Blonde Salad) adds a sporty, playful vibe to a standout dress with a novelty clutch and colorful kicks.

In a Rails shirtdress, Dylanlex necklace and Stuart Weitzman boots with an Elizabeth and James bag.

PLAID SHIRTDRESS & OVER-THE-KNEE BOOTS
Chriselle Lim (The Chriselle Factor) dresses up tomboy staples with a polished blazer and notice-me boots.

In a Chanel dress and sneakers with a Chanel clutch.

SILKY BLOUSE & HAREM PANTS
Kelly Framel (The Glamourai) anchors her flowy look with studded strappy sandals and a top-handle bag.

With a Marc Jacobs bag.

In a Bar III top and skirt.

BLACK TANK TOP & FULL SKIRT
Gabi Gregg's (GabiFresh) statement necklace brings a bright pop of color to her otherwise neutral outfit.

BLOUSE, BOW & CUFFED JEANS
Danielle Bernstein (WeWoreWhat) combines masculine and feminine vibes with a boyish blazer and pretty blouse.

In an Equipment top, J Brand jeans and Saint Laurent by Hedi Slimane bow.

In a Kenzo top, Banana Republic skirt, Tibi belt and Stuart Weitzman heels with a Céline bag.

In a Tory Burch dress with a Gucci purse.

In MiH Jeans jeans.

BELTED COAT, BLOUSE & PRINTED SKIRT

Wendy Nguyen (Wendy's Lookbook) creates a rich mix with patterns and pieces in the same olive palette.

TIE-DYE DRESS & LOAFERS

Blair Eadie (Atlantic-Pacific) adds a relaxed touch to a bold dress with a cross-body bag and tasseled loafers.

CLASSIC SHIRT & WIDE-LEG JEANS

Leandra Medine (Man Repeller) balances fashion-forward denim with a button-up and sandals.

GREAT TIPS FROM **A-LIST** STYLISTS!

From **maximum-impact outfit ideas** to clever ways to **transform your closet,** these tricks are fresh, easy and so helpful

GEORGE KOTSIOPOULOS

Has worked with: **ZOE SALDANA, SANDRA BULLOCK, KRISTEN STEWART**

Make black feel special "Many stars wear color on the red carpet, but Rooney Mara, Zoë Saldana and others love black—it's easy and looks good on everyone. The trick is to make it stand out with texture and details."

Show just enough skin "It's elegant to only expose one or two body parts at a time. When Sandra Bullock wears a minidress, everything else is covered. Also, try gorgeous flats instead of heels— they're chic instead of sexy."

Keep quick fixes handy "Spritz hair spray on your shoes' soles to make them nonslip, and use a touch of nail polish to cover up scuffed heels."

SECRET WEAPON: SHAPEWEAR

"Most celebrities—even the ones you think have perfect bodies—need it. It doesn't matter how beautiful your outfit is, take the time to find shapers to wear under it that really fit, and always go seamless."

look for special black pieces

Zoë Saldana In a Marni dress and Christian Louboutin heels with a Marni clutch.

Lily Collins
In a Barrie
sweater and
Chanel skirt.

mix your patterns!

SECRET WEAPON: A GOOD TAILOR

"You can be wearing the coolest new trends and designers, but if your clothing doesn't fit right, it's a waste. The tailoring can be as simple as cinching the waist of a dress or hemming a pair of pants."

ROB ZANGARDI & MARIEL HAENN

Have worked with: **JENNIFER LOPEZ, SHAKIRA, LILY COLLINS, RACHEL McADAMS**

Figure out your mood "Decide how you're feeling: Edgy? Natural? Elegant? Sexy? Then find one statement piece that really exudes that sort of attitude and build from there."

Break the rules "These days, anything goes. Wear white after Labor Day, mix prints and try combos that aren't supposed to 'work.' Why not?"

Own a can't-miss outfit "Everyone should have a stylish look that always works when you need to get out the door fast. We recommend black or dark skinny jeans, a flowy top and motorcycle boots with a bit of a heel—that's always flattering."

LINDSAY ALBANESE

Has worked with: **BELLA THORNE, ALI LANDRY, KRISTIN CAVALLARI**

Spend wisely "Think about your go-to pieces and update them—if you love your pencil skirt, buy one in a fresh pastel. Use only 25% of your budget on bold trends that get less wear."

Look to social media "Check out street-style and celeb photos for ways to rework what you already own. Maybe you only need to add a new accessory."

Assess your closet "Arrange by category (tops, skirts, dresses and pants) and then by color, so you can clearly see what you have too much or little of. You might be surprised!"

Experiment with a new buy "Don't rip the tags off right away—try the item on with things from your closet. If you can't make at least three outfits or you're just not excited, return it."

SECRET WEAPON: A FITTED BLACK BLAZER "It's versatile, elongating and hides a multitude of figure concerns. Plus, it adds instant polish and sophistication to everything from boyfriend jeans to cocktail dresses."

update your look with pastels!

Bella Thorne In a Bec & Bridge top and skirt and Bionda Castana heels.

add interest with a print clutch

Mandy Moore
In a L'Agence top and Manolo Blahnik heels with a NewbarK clutch.

EMILY CURRENT & MERITT ELLIOTT

Have worked with: **JESSICA ALBA, EMMA ROBERTS, MANDY MOORE**

Punch up basics "Start with classics like perfect-fitting jeans and a white button-up. Then add a bolder piece, whether it's bronze-colored heels, a print clutch or a bright blazer for a point of interest."

Play with proportions "A piece can take on an entirely new life when it's a little baggy or a bit on the smaller side. So take a few different sizes into the dressing room."

Create contrast "To make an impactful look, go for items that are polar opposites—think: a leather jacket over a lace dress, a supershiny shoe with distressed denim."